Gareth's Guide to

SAVING THE ENVIRONMENT

BY JILL KEPPELER

Gareth Stevens
PUBLISHING

Please visit our website, www.garethstevens.com. For a free color catalog of all our high-quality books, call toll free 1-800-542-2595 or fax 1-877-542-2596.

Library of Congress Cataloging-in-Publication Data

Names: Keppeler, Jill, author.
Title: Gareth's guide to saving the environment / Jill Keppeler.
Description: New York : Gareth Stevens Publishing, 2019. | Series: Gareth
    guides to an extraordinary life | Includes index.
Identifiers: LCCN 2018005378| ISBN 9781538220597 (library bound) | ISBN
    9781538220610 (pbk.) | ISBN 9781538220627 (6 pack)
Subjects: LCSH: Environmentalism–Juvenile literature. | Environmental
    protection–Juvenile literature.
Classification: LCC GE195.55 .K46 2019 | DDC 363.7–dc23
LC record available at https://lccn.loc.gov/2018005378

First Edition

Published in 2019 by
Gareth Stevens Publishing
111 East 14th Street, Suite 349
New York, NY 10003

Copyright © 2019 Gareth Stevens Publishing

Editor: Therese Shea

Photo credits: Cover, p. 1 MR.PAPASR MAKEE/Shutterstock.com; cover, pp. 1–32 (background texture) Thiti Saichua/Shutterstock.com; cover, pp. 1–32 (design elements) VDOVINA ELENA/Shutterstock.com; p. 5 Africa Studio/Shutterstock.com; p. 7 Encyclopaedia Britannica/UIG/Getty Images; p. 9 Serjio74/Shutterstock.com; p. 11 William Campbell/Sygma via Getty Images; p. 13 NASA/USGS (http://ga.water. usgs.gov/edu/2010/gallery/global-water-volume.html); p. 15 (both) Bettmann/Getty Images; p. 17 Yoram Lehmann/Photolibrary/Getty Images; p. 19 (top) Climate Strike (https://www.youtube.com/channel/UCcDHR8QbnktP9fLBdCa4rdw)/Neegzistuoja/ Wikipedia.org; p. 19 (bottom) Sean Gallup/Getty Images; p. 21 Dudarev Mikhail/ Shutterstock.com; p. 23 marktucan/Shutterstock.com; p. 25 Ty Wright/Bloomberg via Getty Images; p. 27 Idaho Statesman/Idaho Statesman/MCT via Getty Images; p. 29 Dmytro Zinkevych/Shutterstock.com.

Printed in the United States of America

CPSIA compliance information: Batch #CS18GS: For further information contact Gareth Stevens, New York, New York at 1-800-542-2595.

CONTENTS

WORDS IN THE GLOSSARY APPEAR IN **BOLD** TYPE THE FIRST TIME THEY ARE USED IN THE TEXT.

ONLY ONE PLANET

More than 7 billion people live on this big, beautiful planet we call Earth. It's the only home humankind has ever known, but sometimes we don't take very good care of it. Fortunately, many people are working hard to save and protect Earth and our **environment**. There are scientists, **activists**, writers, and many others who have a role to play. You can work to save the environment, too!

You can study to be an environmental leader when you grow up, but you can also take steps to help now. You can do small things to help Earth, and you can encourage your friends and family to practice these behaviors, too. You can also connect with others interested in making an impact. Activists can be any age!

> ► **SPOTLIGHT!**
> JOBS FOR ENVIRONMENTAL SCIENTISTS ARE EXPECTED TO GROW FASTER THAN MOST JOBS THROUGH 2024!

Special Scientists

Many kinds of scientists work to help Earth and the environment, but environmental scientists specialize in it. Environmental science is a field that covers many different kinds of science, including ecology, engineering, and geology, and uses them to study problems in the environment. Environmental scientists study how humans affect the environment and may also be involved in politics. Interested in becoming an environmental scientist? You'll need to earn at least one college degree.

Many environmental scientists work for state and local governments. Some work in offices, but many work outside in nature.

5

EVERYTHING'S LINKED

It may seem hard to know where to start your efforts to save the environment. The natural world has so many different parts! It's composed of the atmosphere, the hydrosphere, the lithosphere, and the biosphere. The atmosphere is the air, the layer of gases that surround Earth. The hydrosphere is the water, both liquid and frozen, on Earth and the water vapor in the atmosphere. The lithosphere is the outer layer of the planet's surface. It includes both rocks and soil.

The biosphere is the part of the environment that includes all living things and their products. Animals and plants are part of it. So are the people—including you! All the parts of the environment are linked. If we damage one part, the other parts suffer, too.

SPOTLIGHT!

THE "ECO-" IN "ECOSYSTEM" AND "ECOLOGY" MEANS "**HABITAT**" OR "ENVIRONMENT." IT COMES FROM THE LATIN *OECO*, WHICH MEANS "HOUSEHOLD." THIS COMES FROM THE GREEK *OIKOS*, WHICH MEANS "HOUSE."

Excellent Ecosystems

The ecosystem of an area includes all the living and nonliving things in that area. This means things from all four parts of the environment! Ecosystems can be tiny or huge, or any size in between. The living things in each ecosystem all depend on each other to survive. They rely on the nonliving parts, too. For example, ecosystems depend on the sun for their energy. Unfortunately, humans have harmed many of Earth's ecosystems by altering the land for their own purposes.

Earth's Environmental Spheres

Each part of Earth's environment affects the others.

THE WILD KINGDOM

All the parts of the environment are linked, but people working to help Earth often focus on one part. If you love animals, you might want to learn how scientists and activists devote their time to helping protect and rescue Earth's amazing creatures.

Protecting wildlife can mean working to save the animals' habitats from destruction or it can mean protecting the animals themselves from people who would hurt them. Often, it means both! Animals need clean air, food, water, and a safe space to live, just like humans do. Zoologists and other scientists study animals so we can learn to help them in other ways, too. Sometimes we can help bring a species back right from the edge of extinction.

SPOTLIGHT!

ANIMAL SPECIES CAN BECOME EXTINCT NATURALLY, BUT THE WORLD WILDLIFE FUND (WWF) ESTIMATES THAT THE CURRENT RATE OF EXTINCTION IS 100 TO 1,000 TIMES HIGHER THAN IT SHOULD BE.

The Endangered Species Act

On December 28, 1973, President Richard Nixon signed the **Endangered** Species Act (ESA). This law called for the conservation of endangered and threatened species. Many kinds of animals became protected under the act, and 99 percent of the species that have been named on it are still around. This is a valuable law for helping animals in danger. You can help them by writing to your political representatives and telling them just how important you think the ESA is!

1967 → year bald eagles are listed as endangered

400 → estimated breeding pairs of bald eagles left in 1973

2007 → year bald eagles are removed from endangered list

10,000 → estimated bald eagle breeding pairs as of 2017

One of the species helped by the Endangered Species Act is the bald eagle. The act's protection helped these big, beautiful birds recover so much that they were removed from the ESA in 2007.

THE STORY OF THE GRAY WOLF

The comeback of the gray wolf is a great example of how saving an animal can also help its ecosystem. In the early days of the United States, people hunted the wolf so much that by the early to mid-1900s, it was nearly extinct. Many wolves once lived in Yellowstone National Park in the United States, but by 1926, people had killed the last wolf pack there.

In the 1990s, however, conservationists started the Yellowstone Wolf Project. They caught wolves in Canada and other locations and released them in the park. People protected them and kept track of their movements. By December 2016, there were about 11 packs of wolves in Yellowstone and more than 100 wolves. They've helped biodiversity in the park in many ways.

9.8 → average number of wolves in a wolf pack in Yellowstone

> **SPOTLIGHT!**
> SOME WILDLIFE ORGANIZATIONS ALLOW YOU TO "ADOPT" AN ENDANGERED ANIMAL BY GIVING MONEY TO THE ORGANIZATION. YOU WON'T GET A REAL GRAY WOLF, BUT THE ORGANIZATION MIGHT SEND YOU A STUFFED ANIMAL!

Biodiversity and Yellowstone

Biodiversity is the variety of native plants and animals in an ecosystem. These organisms affect each other. In Yellowstone, because the wolves were back, elk populations started to shrink. This meant certain trees that elk would eat had the opportunity to grow. The rise in healthy adult trees helped animals that depended on them, including beavers. Beaver dams created pools that aided small animals. The return of the wolves also helped animals that eat the kills wolves leave behind.

Doug Smith, leader of the Yellowstone Wolf Project, is shown with a captured wolf. "Most ecosystems are best when they're balanced," he said, "and I think it's safe to say that Yellowstone without wolves . . . affected the balance of the ecosystem."

FRESHWATER, SALT WATER

All life on Earth depends on water to survive. Earth's oceans, which cover more than 70 percent of the planet, are essential to a healthy environment. Tiny ocean plants called phytoplankton provide about half the oxygen we need to live! The oceans also absorb a large amount of carbon dioxide, a **greenhouse gas** that can cause global warming and **climate change**.

The saltwater oceans are important, but much of the life on Earth also needs freshwater. We need freshwater to drink, and many animals can only live in freshwater. More than 100,000 species depend on freshwater ecosystems. However, only a small amount of Earth's water is fresh. That makes it important to conserve this water and keep it safe and clean.

> **SPOTLIGHT!**
> MORE THAN 40 PERCENT OF ALL FISH SPECIES LIVE IN FRESHWATER.

Less Than 1 Percent

About 97 percent of the water on Earth is in the oceans. This is salt water. Of the freshwater remaining, most—nearly 69 percent—is frozen in glaciers and polar ice. About 30 percent is groundwater, which is water deep within Earth's soil and rock. Only about 0.3 percent of freshwater is available on Earth's surface! Most of this—about 87 percent—is stored in lakes. About 11 percent is in swamps, and 2 percent is in rivers.

The water table is the upper limit of the part of the ground that's full of freshwater. In 2017, scientist Jay Famiglietti warned, "The water table is dropping all over the world. There's not an infinite supply of water." The image below represents the amounts of all water and freshwater on Earth in relation to the size of our planet.

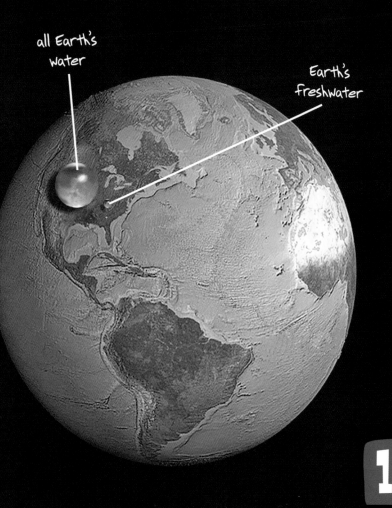

all Earth's water

Earth's freshwater

THE BURNING RIVER

Pollution from chemicals, garbage, and other wastes threatens our oceans and freshwater supplies. Environmental scientists and activists work to protect Earth's waters. Part of their job is to convince people in power, such as politicians, to ask for, write, and pass laws to help.

The Cuyahoga River is a river in northeast Ohio, near Lake Erie, one of the Great Lakes. About 50 years ago, the river was thick with pollution, including waste from factories and sewage from cities. In fact, trash floating in the water sometimes caught fire. The idea of a river so polluted it could burn upset many people. They demanded action! The burning river led, in part, to the creation of the Environmental Protection Agency (EPA) and the Clean Water Act.

13

→ number of times the Cuyahoga River caught fire between 1868 and 1969

> ### SPOTLIGHT!
> PEOPLE WHO SAW THE CUYAHOGA RIVER IN THE 1950S AND 1960S SAID IT OOZED RATHER THAN FLOWED! THE RIVER WAS DESCRIBED AS BIOLOGICALLY DEAD.

Ohio Environmentalists

Carl Stokes was the mayor of Cleveland, Ohio, from 1967 to 1971. He was the first African American mayor of a major US city and got national attention because of that. He used that publicity to get people to pay attention to Cleveland's problem with water pollution. He worked with his brother Louis Stokes, a member of the US House of Representatives, to help get new laws passed, including the Clean Water Act of 1972.

This picture, which ran in *Time* magazine in 1969, shows a Cuyahoga River fire in the 1950s. Today, the Cuyahoga is much cleaner, although there is still pollution.

IN THE AIR

Just like all living things need water to survive, all living things also need air. Clean air is important for our health. It's essential to keep the whole planet healthy, too! Pollution in the air can make people, animals, and plants sick. It can cause breathing problems and hurt people's lungs. It also contributes to global warming and climate change. It's another focus in your fight to save the environment.

Air pollution comes from many sources, including vehicles, homes, and businesses. It's composed of gases and particles in the air that affect the climate and hurt living creatures. Primary pollutants are gases and particles that enter the air directly. Secondary pollutants are pollutants that are created when primary pollutants react with things in the atmosphere.

SPOTLIGHT!

NATURAL SOURCES CAN PRODUCE AIR POLLUTION, TOO. VOLCANOES AND FOREST FIRES CAN BOTH SET LOOSE GREAT AMOUNTS OF PARTICLES AND GASES!

Fossil Fuels

The burning of fossil fuels causes much of Earth's air pollution. Fossil fuels are matter formed over millions of years from plant or animal remains. This matter is then burned for power. Coal, oil, and natural gas are all fossil fuels. Because it takes so long for fossil fuels to form, they're considered a nonrenewable resource. There could be more someday, but that's very far in the future!

In the 1980s, a steel mill in Provo, Utah, closed for months because of a strike. Later, a study by researcher Arden Pope showed that hospital admissions for kids with **respiratory** problems dropped by a third while the mill was closed because it wasn't releasing metallic particles into the air.

JULIANA V. UNITED STATES

Some environmental activists fight through the US court system. In 2015, a group of 21 young people, then 9 to 20 years old, filed a lawsuit against the US government for not doing enough to work against the use of fossil fuels. As of early 2018, the case was still in progress.

Avery McRae, the second youngest in the group, said the case will affect the future of kids around the world. It may decide "if they're going to have to wear air masks every time they go outside or if they're going to live in **pristine** environments where they can swim in cold water in the summer and fish and hike in old-growth forests and not worry about climate change," she explained in a 2017 interview with the *Atlantic*.

SPOTLIGHT!

AVERY MCRAE HAD HER FIRST TASTE OF ACTIVISM AFTER SHE READ A BOOK ABOUT SNOW LEOPARDS. CONCERNED THEY WERE ENDANGERED, SHE HELD A FUNDRAISER AND **DONATED** $200 TO THE SNOW LEOPARD TRUST.

Earth Guardian

Xiuhtezcatl Roske-Martinez is another one of the young people involved with *Juliana v. United States*. He's also the youth director of the environmental awareness group Earth Guardians. Roske-Martinez gave his first public speech at age 6. "When I was 5 years old, I wanted to go to all the factories and shut them down," he said. "But once I turned 6, I realized that it was us that were buying from the factories."

The group involved in *Juliana v. United States*, including Roske-Martinez (pictured here), says the government is **jeopardizing** their future by not taking climate change seriously.

Climate activist James Hansen and his granddaughter Sophie Kivlehan, another of the 21 young people who filed the lawsuit *Juliana v. United States*, speak to the press at a United Nations Climate Change Conference in 2017.

DEFORESTATION DAMAGE

In your fight for the environment, don't forget about plants! Plants give us things to eat, but also do a lot of good for the environment. Plants take in carbon dioxide, which helps fight global warming. They use this gas and sunlight to produce food for themselves and give off oxygen, which we need to breathe. Plants also provide food and homes for animals.

Sadly, humans have done a lot of damage to Earth's plants. People cut and burn down trees and remove plants from land to build homes and businesses and plant crops. This is called deforestation. According to the Food and Agriculture Organization of the United Nations, people cut down about 18 million acres (7.3 million ha) of forest every year and have cleared about half the planet's tropical forests.

20 TO 30 YEARS

→ number of years it takes a growing oak tree to produce seeds

> **→ SPOTLIGHT!**
> TREES ARE A RENEWABLE RESOURCE, BUT THEY NEED TO BE REPLANTED AND IT TAKES TIME FOR THEM TO GROW.

Coping with Carbon

Forests act as a carbon sink, which means they absorb more carbon dioxide from the atmosphere than they give off. Some of this carbon dioxide is used in photosynthesis, but trees also store some of it. When trees or other green plants die, they release their stored carbon. With deforestation, not only do we lose the positive effect of the living trees, we also get an increase in carbon dioxide in the atmosphere from the dead trees.

Trees are important to Earth's water systems. They absorb rainfall and release water vapor through their leaves. However, forests are being cut down at a worrying rate in parts of the world.

SAVING THE RAIN FOREST

Deforestation is a worldwide problem, but tropical rain forests are particularly at risk. About 80 percent of the animal species we know of live in these **biomes**, making them home to much of the planet's biodiversity. Still, people have destroyed about 17 percent of the Amazon rain forest over the past 50 years.

Back in 1999, Janine Licare and Aislin Livingstone were only 9 years old when they decided they needed to do something to help protect the rain forest in their home of Costa Rica in Central America. The girls created an organization called Kids Saving the Rainforest to educate people and raise money. The nonprofit organization is still growing today! It runs a wildlife rescue center and **sanctuary** in Costa Rica and also plants trees.

90

percentage of forests in the continental US removed since 1600

SPOTLIGHT!

TO BE CONSIDERED A RAIN FOREST, A FOREST MUST RECEIVE AT LEAST 100 INCHES (254 CM) OF RAIN A YEAR.

Starting Small

Licare and Livingstone were children when they had the idea to start their organization. They sold crafts to earn money for their project. Licare, now grown and a college graduate, still serves as the secretary of the Kids Saving the Rainforest organization today. "When your backyard is being torn apart in front of your own eyes," she said in an interview about the group, "anyone would be compelled to try and save it."

The Amazon region in Brazil has the largest rain forest in the world. There are thousands of animals, such as the jaguar shown here, and tens of thousands of species of plants.

OUR MOTHER EARTH

Just like pollution can harm Earth's air and water, it can also damage Earth's soil and rock. Chemicals from factories and **landfills** can leak into the ground and **contaminate** it. Mines and farms can also release chemicals that can harm Earth and make people, plants, and animals ill.

To prevent this from happening, governments can create laws to limit what chemicals businesses can use and how they must be disposed of. You can write your representatives and ask them to support laws like this. You can also make sure you're careful about what you throw away and how you get rid of it. Everything you throw away has to go somewhere. Often, it goes into a landfill.

258 MILLION TONS (234 MILLION MT)

→ amount of garbage produced by Americans in 2014

> **SPOTLIGHT!**
> ACCORDING TO THE ENVIRONMENTAL PROTECTION AGENCY, AMERICANS PRODUCE MORE THAN 4 POUNDS (1.8 KG) OF WASTE PER PERSON PER DAY!

The Problem of Landfills

Landfills accomplish an important purpose: they hold many things we throw away. However, they're a big problem, too. They use up land that could be left wild for animals, plants, and people. They give off greenhouse gases and may release toxins, or poisons. More than half the waste people throw away ends up in landfills. One way to help the environment is to throw away less that could wind up there.

Waste that ends up in landfills takes a very long time to break down. Some hardly breaks down at all!

EARTH DAY

Recycling isn't a new idea, and people didn't always throw away so much. When goods were more difficult to produce and obtain, people were better at reusing them and finding new things to do with them. But after World War II (1939–1945), when goods became more plentiful and cost less, things changed. "The idea that you threw stuff out when it wore out is a 20th-century idea," author Susan Strasser said in a 2016 interview with *Time* magazine.

Ideas changed again in the 1960s and 1970s, when the modern environmental movement started. In 1970, Senator Gaylord Nelson of Wisconsin, who was very involved with environmental causes, proposed a day for people to speak out about the environment. This became Earth Day, which people still celebrate every April 22.

> ## SPOTLIGHT!
> NELSON'S FIRST ENVIRONMENTAL CAMPAIGN, BEGUN WHEN HE WAS 14, WAS A PLAN TO PLANT TREES ALONG ROADS NEAR HIS HOMETOWN. IT WAS DEFEATED, BUT NELSON KEPT TRYING TO HELP THE ENVIRONMENT.

Unity of Purpose

Nelson's Earth Day got people excited about helping protect the environment. He created it because he was concerned citizens didn't have a "unity of purpose," something to pull them together to help the planet. He said he needed to "get the nation to wake up and pay attention to the most important challenge the human species faces on the planet." Earth Day helped do this. People now mark the day in many other countries as well.

20 MILLION

estimated number of Americans who celebrated the first Earth Day

Like Carl Stokes in Cleveland, Gaylord Nelson used his political position to draw attention to environmental issues. It marked the start of a time in which people created many environmental laws and began modern recycling programs.

TAKING YOUR OWN STEPS

Hopefully, you now understand there are many ways to work toward saving the environment. Scientists do research to learn more about it and figure out ways to protect it. As a reporter or author, you could write about the importance of protecting the environment and tell the inspiring stories of those who do. You could also run for office and become a politician who pushes for new environmental protection laws.

But you don't have to wait until you grow up! There's a lot you can do now. You can make sure your family and your school reuse and recycle as much as possible. You can conserve water at your home. You can write to your elected representatives and tell them how important the environment is to you. Every movement starts somewhere!

> **SPOTLIGHT!**
> WHEN YOU OUTGROW A BOOK OR TOY, DON'T THROW IT AWAY! GIVE IT TO SOMEONE ELSE OR DONATE IT TO A GROUP THAT SELLS OR GIVES AWAY USED GOODS.

Powerful Words

Rachel Carson (1907-1964) was an author who helped spark the environmental movement. She worked as a biologist for the US government before becoming known as a writer who was skilled at explaining scientific concepts to a wide range of people. Her most famous book was *Silent Spring*, published in 1962, in which she warned that chemicals called pesticides could spread throughout the food chain, harming plants, animals, and people.

TIPS FOR SAVING THE ENVIRONMENT

> Bring reusable bags when shopping to cut down on plastic and paper waste.

> Encourage your family to use natural cleaning products to reduce chemical pollution.

> Reuse as many items as you can to avoid adding to landfills.

> Walk or ride a bike instead of taking a car that releases air pollutants.

> Turn off lights when you're not using them because electricity is often produced with fossil fuels.

> Drink tap water to reduce plastic bottle waste.

> Turn off water while you're brushing your teeth to conserve freshwater.

> Start a garden because foods in stores are transported by vehicles that use fossil fuels.

> Research more ways to save the environment and get others involved!

Even kids can help save the environment.
What will you do to help?

GLOSSARY

activist: a person who acts strongly in support of or against an issue

biome: a natural community of plants and animals, such as a forest or desert

climate change: long-term change in Earth's climate, caused partly by human activities such as burning oil and natural gas

contaminate: to pollute something

donate: to give something to others who need it

endangered: in danger of dying out

environment: the conditions that surround a living thing and affect the way it lives

greenhouse gas: a gas in the atmosphere that traps heat there

habitat: the natural place where an animal or plant lives

jeopardize: to expose to danger or risk

landfill: a place where garbage is buried

pristine: not spoiled or polluted

respiratory: having to do with respiration, or the movement of air into and out of the lungs

sanctuary: a place of safety and protection

FOR MORE INFORMATION

Books

Cohn, Jessica. *Hand to Earth: Saving the Environment.* Huntington Beach, CA: Teacher Created Materials, 2013.

Elliott, Marion. *Recycled Craft Projects for Kids.* Helotes, TX: Armadillo Children's Publishing, 2014.

Meeker, Clare Hodgson. *Rhino Rescue! and More True Stories of Saving Animals.* Washington, DC: National Geographic, 2016.

Websites

How You Can Help!
pbskids.org/zoom/activities/action/way04.html
Learn what kids like you are doing to help the environment.

Kids Saving the Rainforest
www.kidssavingtherainforest.org/
See what the Kids Saving the Rainforest organization is doing today.

Mission Animal Rescue
kids.nationalgeographic.com/explore/nature/mission-animal-rescue/
Find out how you can help endangered animals.

INDEX